The
English
Landscape
Garden

The English Landscape Garden

David Jarrett

Academy Editions · London

ACKNOWLEDGEMENTS

I thank the following for their permission to reproduce material from their collections: Aerofilms, London p.23 (top), p.68, p.70 (bottom), p.92 (top); The Bodleian Library, Oxford p.42 (top), p.43, p.46 (bottom), p.49 (top left), p.50 (top), p.51, p.52 (top), pp.134-137; The British Library, London p.11, p.19, p.28, p.46 (top), p.57, p.64, p.65, p.70 (top), p.80, p.82, p.118 (top); The National Gallery, London p.8; The National Portrait Gallery, London p.12, p.66. All other photographs are by the author.

My thanks for their help and cooperation also go to Thomas Byrom, Mary Jarrett, John Kerruish, Jean Ruzicka and Thomas Upcher.

**To the memory of
MAL DEAN 1941-1974**

Front cover
Kew, a view across Brown's lake with Syon House in the distance.

Frontispiece
Melbourne Hall, a view from the house.

Page 6
Blenheim, showing Vanbrugh's bridge and Brown's lake.

First published in Great Britain in 1978 by
Academy Editions, 7 Holland Street, London W8

SBN 85670-1734

Printed and bound in Great Britain by Balding & Mansell Ltd., Wisbech

CONTENTS

INTRODUCTION

"The sweetness that all longed for night and day . . ."

Surely among a rich man's flowering lawns,
Amid the rustle of his planted hills,
Life overflows without ambitious pains;
And rains down life until the basin spills,
And mounts more dizzy high the more it rains
As though to choose whatever shape it wills
And never stoop to a mechanical
Or servile shape, at others' beck and call.

Mere dreams, mere dreams . . .

W.B. Yeats

The ancestral home, like Lady Gregory's eighteenth century Coole Park, stands as an ideal of civilised calm at the beginning of Yeats's *Meditations in Time of Civil War* (1921). Yeats is yearningly responsive to that ideal, but recognises its illusory quality. His feeling recalls that of the eighteenth century Mr. Pyncheon in Nathaniel Hawthorne's *The House of the Seven Gables* (1851) who, when particularly hard pressed by problems relating to land greed in the New World, contemplates wistfully a landscape by Claude that hangs on his wall. The painting, showing "a shadowy and sun-streaked vista penetrat[ing] . . . remotely into an ancient wood", is the vehicle by which Pyncheon tries "to bring back sunny recollections". It represents for him a golden age of the Old World, an idealised setting suggestive of Virgil's *Georgics* and *Aeneid,* rendered pleasingly melancholy and picturesque in its evocation of the Ruins of Rome. Had Pyncheon been living in England he might have been able to look not on his wall but through his window to see such a poetic landscape, and by walking in the artfully contrived pleasure-grounds at Stourhead he could have fulfilled his desire to enter the Claudian landscape. Pyncheon is a man of refined poetic sensibility, but Hawthorne involves him in a bitter and violent struggle over his estates. Yeats's poem goes on to consider the relation between the ancestral home and such violence:

Some violent bitter man, some powerful man
Called architect and artist in, that they,
Bitter and violent men, might rear in stone
The sweetness that all longed for night and day,
The gentleness that none had ever known.

None of the gardeners with whom I shall be concerned can be described as violent and bitter. Indeed Lancelot Brown (1716-1783) and Humphry Repton (1752-1818) appear to have been extremely attractive characters, if somewhat snobbish or opinionated at times. Similarly some of the aristocratic patrons of the gardeners, like Lord Cobham who

Claude Lorrain, *Coast View of Delos with Aeneas* (National Gallery, London). Claude's paintings had a profound effect upon the taste of eighteenth century English landscapists. This painting has a particular relationship with Henry Hoare's Stourhead where the disposition of the Palladian bridge, the Pantheon and the Temple of Flora echoes that of bridge and temples in Claude's landscape.

transformed Stowe, probably came near to deserving some of the encomiums lavished upon them by Pope, James Thomson, and lesser poets. But it remains striking and to some, no doubt, sinister that an age of flagrant political corruption and jobbery, particularly under Sir Robert Walpole, and of generally rigid ideas of social class (even Repton believed it wrong to teach the lower orders how to read) should have seen the creation of so many ideal naturalised landscape parks. Certainly the landscapes, including Brown's, can have an unpleasant or just flippant aspect. The typical Brown park, in which an imposing Palladian building is isolated in an expanse of grass relieved by clumps of trees and reflected in the smooth surface of a lake, demonstrates the tendency of the Whig aristocracy to cut themselves off in their grandeur from the village. And if Lord Cobham was not much criticised at the time for shifting the whole village of Stowe (*c.*1730) some two miles because it impeded plans for improving his grounds, it is still obvious that his action might have been anti-social. Later, in 1760, when that "marvel of pomposity and propriety", as Horace Walpole called the first Lord Harcourt, wished to extend his pleasure gardens at Nuneham Courtenay he felt it necessary to remove the village of Nuneham more than a mile away and to replace its Gothic parish church with an impractical classical temple — almost certainly providing Oliver Goldsmith with the model of anti-social behaviour depicted in *The Deserted Village* (1770):

> Thus fares the land by luxury betrayed;
> In Nature's simplest charms at first arrayed,
> But verging to decline, its splendours rise,
> Its vistas strike, its palaces surprise;
> While, scourged by famine from the smiling land,

> The mournful peasant leads his humble band,
> And while he sinks, without one arm to save,
> The country blooms — a garden and a grave.

If Goldsmith's scene appears a little overpainted, at least it rings truer than the answering poem by William Whitehead written in the following year. It begins:

> The careful matrons of the plain
> Had left their cots without a sigh
> Well pleased to house their little train
> In happier mansions warm and dry.

However, it is not my intention to stress anti-social or flippant aspects of the eighteenth century landscape garden. It is important to acknowledge that they exist, just as it is important to know that, as Christopher Hussey points out, the desire to economise and to hunt played no small part in causing the removal of formalised box trees and exotic plants from royal gardens early in the eighteenth century, or that enclosure and the consequent agricultural revolution had a dramatic effect upon the development of landscape gardening. But to emphasise escapism or the English talent for compromise in connection with the landscape movement is, I think, misleading. Whatever his dependence upon aristocratic patronage, there must have been something grandly uncompromising about "Capability" Brown which allowed him to transform the English landscape on such a scale and according to such consistent values. If we look for escape and compromise in the subject we shall find examples of it, but then we shall be in danger of missing the true nobility, utility, and idealism of the English landscape garden. Since Romanticism we have grown accustomed to associating art with an organic principle of growth; these gardens are works of art, and as such they can speak directly to us and liberate us — however interested we may be in history and topography — from time and space. It is with the artistic effect that I am concerned ultimately, though first we shall turn to the history of the subject.

There is something practical and noble, as well as anxiously escapist, in the way that nineteenth century England adopted, like a Yeatsian mask, the persona of medievalism in the Houses of Parliament by Sir Charles Barry and A. W. Pugin, in William Dyce's Arthurian paintings in the Queen's Robing Room there or in Tennyson's *Idylls of the King*. There is a great deal of the first two qualities and far less anxiety in the picturesque mask, be it Augustan, Virgilian, Claudian or whatever, that the eighteenth century landscapists erected on such a grand scale for the face of the country.

The Lake at Stourhead, showing the Palladian bridge and the Pantheon.

William Hogarth, "The Rake's Levée", *The Rakes Progress* (1735).

The Gardeners

The second plate of William Hogarth's *The Rake's Progress* (1735) depicts the *levée* of young Tom Rakewell who is just beginning to launch himself on his career as a fashionable, rich London blade. He is surrounded therefore by all those whose services he can buy to further that end. Lichtenberg, with suitable irony, identifies most of them in his *Commentaries on Hogarth* (1784-96). A Frenchified dancing-master leers ingratiatingly and foppishly describes with his body a parody of Hogarth's own serpentine line of beauty. An ox-like English cudgel expert stares balefully at the more delicate French fencing-master, while at the keyboard is, perhaps, Handel himself. Flowing like a pianola roll from the back of the latter's chair is a list of the gifts that were lavished upon the Italian *castrato* Signor Farinelli who was enchanting fashionable London at the time; one of his lady admirers is even reported to have called ecstatically "One God, one Farinelli!" from her box at one of his performances. Hogarth's sturdy and ironic common sense made him a determined apologist for the native tradition, and foreign imports like the Italian opera seemed to him strained and trifling in their graces. It is a particular sign of Rakewell's bad taste that he turns away from the sad figure behind his right shoulder to the thug on his left who is offering himself to help the Rake in affairs of "honour"; for the person seemingly rejected is Charles Bridgeman (1680?-1738), the gardener whose works early in the eighteenth century took some of the first significant steps towards the naturalised landscape which was to become known and widely imitated in Europe and America as the English Garden.

The story of how Englishmen of taste in the eighteenth century moved toward an aesthetic acceptance of the principle of irregularity in nature and then in art has often been told. Many are familiar with Steele's dismissal of the art of topiary as an absurd restraint of nature, with Addison's similar liking for the natural tree or with Shaftesbury's declaration of the value of

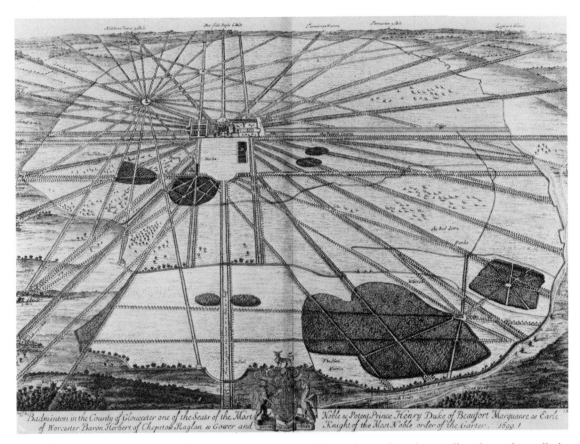

Badminton, Gloucestershire, in the seventeenth century. There is an obsessive quality about the radiating straight avenues in this layout. It is possible that Capability Brown played some part in the naturalising of the park in the eighteenth century.

rugged and picturesque elements in landscape. The influential Addison in *Spectator* 14 (1712) said:

> I do not know whether I am singular in my Opinion, but for my part I would rather look upon a tree in all its Luxuriancy and Diffusion of Boughs and Branches, than when it is . . . cut and trimmed into a Mathematical Figure; and cannot but fancy that an Orchard in Flower looks infinitely more delightful than all the little Labyrinths of the most finished Parterre.

Two years earlier the third Earl of Shaftesbury, equally influential in the first half of the eighteenth century, allowed one of the participants in his dialogue *The Moralists* (1710) the following enthusiastic exclamation — particularly striking from the pen of one whose deist common sense made him generally hostile to manifestations of enthusiasm:

> I shall no longer resist the passion in me for things of a natural kind; where neither Art, nor the Conceit or Caprice of Man has spoil'd their genuine Order by breaking in upon the Primitive State. Even the rude Rocks, the mossy Caverns, the irregular unwrought Grotto's and broken Falls of waters, with all the horrid graces of the Wilderness itself, as representing NATURE more, will be the more engaging, and appear with a magnificence beyond the mockery of princely gardens.

A glance at Bridgeman's design for the grounds at Stowe will show that he was not in ardent pursuit of "all the horrid graces of the Wilderness", but there remains here enough emphasis on the irregular and the serpentine to indicate why Bridgeman can be regarded as the initiator of the first important reaction against the Dutch-influenced formal gardens with clipped evergreen hedges and rectangular beds, and against the geometric grandeur of

Gawen Hamilton, *A Conversation of Virtuosis* (National Portrait Gallery). In this painting of a club of eighteenth century artists can be seen Charles Bridgeman, fifth from the left, and William Kent, second from the right.

gardens influenced by Charles Le Nôtre's achievement at Versailles, imposing symmetrical parterres and radiating straight lines over the landscape. A modest but well-preserved example of a garden in the style of Le Nôtre can be seen at Melbourne Hall, Derbyshire; it was laid out in the late seventeenth and early eighteenth centuries by George London and Henry Wise, the royal gardeners and sometime colleagues of Bridgeman. There is an element of the Dutch manner at Powis Castle, Powis, though the inspiration here is for the most part Italian. The English Garden reverses the process which spreads geometric architectural order from the house into the grounds and attempts instead to draw the graces of the surrounding landscape into the garden itself. Of this development Horace Walpole in *On Modern Gardening* (1770), says:

> . . . the capital stroke, the leading step to all that has followed, was (I believe the first thought was Bridgeman's) the destruction of walls for boundaries, and the invention of fosses — an attempt then deemed so astonishing that the common people called them Ha! Ha's! to express their surprise at finding a sudden and unperceived check to their walk.

In fact, the haha was not invented by Bridgeman, though it was in some form used by him. Usually in the eighteenth century it was a wedge-shaped ditch, four or more feet deep, with a vertical stone wall sunk on the house side. Animals could thus be kept away from the house without fence, wall, or hedge being visible, making possible such impressively long uninterrupted vistas as that to the south of Stowe House. The haha became an indispensable part of the typical Capability Brown landscape, since it was his principle to take turf right up to the house front itself. Towards the end of the century Humphry Repton relaxed this rule and commonsensically accepted the fence in cases where the pretence that housegarden and park are the same was the more unnatural alternative.

Lord Cobham's well-preserved Stowe is one of the most important landscape gardens of the eighteenth century partly because it was created to be something much more than merely a pleasant retreat, partly because it exerted such wide influence, and partly because it employed not only Charles Bridgeman, but also William Kent and Capability Brown — most of the great landscape gardeners of the century, in fact. Cobham, who began with Bridgeman to transform his grounds early in the second decade of the century, was a man of wide culture, a member of the Kit-Kat club and companion therefore of men like Pope, Vanbrugh, and Addison. He was also a staunch Whig, though bitterly opposed to the Whig Prime Minister Sir Robert Walpole. It was while Cobham was not in office because of this opposition that he turned Stowe into an expression of his "High Whiggery" and of his cultural values generally. The political implications of the eighteenth century Englishman's turn toward nature were as obvious to him as they are to us. Le Nôtre's grandiose formalism at Versailles seemed an expression of absolutism, of tyranny, while the British love of unrestrained nature was taken to reflect a basic love of liberty. The English Garden thus became a constitutional taste, like the preference for Shakespeare, wild and unruled according to eighteenth century critical conventions, over the more correct, neo-classic Racine, or, sometimes, for the Gothic style of building over the Palladian. The grounds at Stowe are to be read like a poem or a painting and the temples and other monuments, designed by men such as Vanbrugh, Kent, and James Gibbs, are positioned not just to be picturesque, but to explain Cobham's ideals. So, for example, the Temple of Ancient Virtue, facing the Monument to British Worthies across an atmospheric and painterly rendering of the river Styx, stood close by the Temple of Modern Virtue which was in ruins to symbolise the corruption of public life under Walpole's administration. There is an element of escapism, as in Hawthorne's Mr. Pyncheon, in Cobham's reverence for the classical past, as well as pleasing touches of humour in the arrangement of the grounds. But these do not vitiate the seriousness of the moral idealism expressed; rather, they throw it into relief. The eighteenth century took seriously the moral definition of man in terms of his landscape surroundings, as is evident for example in James Thomson's celebration of Lord Cobham at Stowe or of George Lyttleton at Hagley in *The Seasons* (1726-30). Lyttleton was, in part, the model for Squire Allworthy in Henry Fielding's *Tom Jones* (1749), and Fielding devotes a long and uncharacteristically enthusiastic passage to a description of Allworthy's country seat and its spectacular surroundings. The other model for Allworthy, interestingly enough, was Ralph Allen, whose Prior Park at Bath, featuring one of the earliest Palladian bridges in England, was splendidly landscaped if not by Brown himself then much in his manner. Towards the end of the eighteenth century the romances of Ann Radcliffe consistently represent moral stature through response to landscape.

William Kent (1684-1748), who succeeded Bridgeman at Stowe, was the protégé of the Lord Burlington to whom Pope's *Epistle IV* (1731) of his *Moral Essays* is addressed and who was largely responsible for popularising Palladian standards and designs in English architecture. Kent was a man of many parts, being painter, architect, interior decorator and landscape gardener. Not all that he did was necessarily of the first order, but for his gardening Walpole had high praise. Though *On Modern Gardening* might leave something to be desired in historical scope and accuracy, it remains unsurpassed for its evocation of the special quality of the eighteenth century English landscape garden, and this is nowhere more evident than in the tribute to Kent. The following paragraphs show how well Walpole understood the kind of movement, variety, and harmony for which the landscape gardeners strove. The way in which the passage seems to set a landscape in motion recalls the ambitious descriptions in Thomson's *The Seasons,* a poem which sometimes, like the gardens, deliberately imitates and rivals the landscape paintings of Claude, Gaspar Poussin or the wilder Salvator Rosa; the echoes of Pope's *Epistle to Burlington* are more obvious. Walpole is not entirely misrepresenting Kent here, either, of whom he says that he was

> . . . painter enough to taste the charms of landscape, bold and opinionative enough to dare and to dictate, and born with a genius to strike out a great system from the twilight of imperfect essays. He leaped the fence, and saw that all nature was a garden. He felt the delicious contrast of hill and valley changing imperceptibly into each other, tasted the beauty of the gentle swell, or concave scoop, and remarked how loose groves marked an easy eminence with happy ornament; and while they called in the distant view between their graceful stems, removed and extended the perspective by delusive comparison.
>
> Thus the pencil of his imagination bestowed all the arts of landscape on the scenes he handled. The great principles on which he worked were perspective, and light and shade. Groups of trees broke too uniform or too extensive a lawn; evergreens and woods were opposed to the glare of the champaign; and where the view was less fortunate, or so much exposed as to be beheld at once, he blotted out some parts by thick shades, to divide it into variety, or to make the richest scene more enchanting by reserving it to a farther advance of the spectator's step. Thus selecting favourite objects, and veiling deformities by screens of plantation; sometimes allowing the rudest waste to add its foil to the richest theatre, he realised the compositions of the greatest masters in painting. Where objects were wanting to animate his horizon, his taste as an architect could bestow immediate termination. His buildings, his seats, his temples, were more the works of his pencil than his compasses. We owe the restoration of Greece and the diffusion of architecture to his skill in landscape.

Walpole continues by detailing Kent's skill in handling serpentine streams and in his use of trees, and the quality of the writing remains evocative. The features that Walpole singles out for praise can still be seen at Rousham in Oxfordshire, the finest surviving garden by Kent. Here the winding Cherwell harmonises with Kent's rendering of an Elysium or a Tempe, based partly on his familiarity with the Roman *campagna* and with Italian Renaissance gardens, and his landscape is enriched by temples, statues of satyrs and classical deities, by a modest cascade and by vistas over the Oxfordshire countryside. He has indeed animated his horizon where "objects were wanting" with a large "eye-catcher", a triple-arched façade on a distant hill, while rather nearer to the garden he transformed a mill house into a temple to blend with his landscape. Kent also made use of the judiciously placed clump of trees that was to become a distinguishing feature of Brown's work.

In some ways Walpole's praise for the grandeur of Kent's achievement would be better applied to Brown, for it was he who raised the art of landscape gardening to heroic scale. No doubt his lack of training as anything but a gardener facilitated this, for ultimately there is something limiting about constant allusion to painting, poetry, and mythology in landscape art, forcing one to rely on statuary and architectural monuments. The elements of Brown's ideal landscape are simple; great sweeps of greensward, relieved by clumps of trees, extending right up to the house itself and sloping down to a level sheet of water often ingeniously created from diminutive streams, and a belt of trees encircling the whole park, sometimes opening vistas on to the surrounding country and always rescued from seeming tediously confining by irregularity. The noble simplicity of Brown's vision doubtless contributed much to the unprecedented extent of his operations in remodelling great parks, even when heavy expenditure was necessary by landowners who could rarely expect to live to see their landscape garden in its maturity. The boast implied in Brown's refusal to go to Ireland to work because he had not yet finished England is altogether understandable. His famous nickname was bestowed upon him because of his habit of referring, one imagines with grave dignity, to the "capabilities", or the potential for remodelling, of the parks on which he was consulted. Brown did not have to wait long for success, and ten years after Lord Cobham's death the former head-gardener of Stowe enjoyed such a reputation that he could send his son to Eton, and receive no complaints when his alterations to Vanbrugh's Blenheim were carried out at a cost of £30,000. It was Brown, of course, who took the grass up to the palace at Blenheim and dispensed with the formal parterres. He also created lakes to match Vanbrugh's massive bridge which had formerly thrown its great span across a straight and very narrow canal.

Owing to his enormous influence and success Brown naturally came in for attack during his own lifetime and later. His rival William Chambers, whose work now stands alongside that of Brown at Kew, argued whimsically and sometimes bitterly for greater variety in garden design in works like *A Dissertation on Oriental Gardening* (1772), and there is certainly some justice in his desire for more colourful planting in the eighteenth century garden. After Brown's death his landscape ideal was attacked by exponents of the picturesque school like Sir Uvedale Price and Richard Payne Knight, who demanded more painterly attention to the dramatic ruggedness and grotesqueness of nature. Brown's smoothness seemed to them tedious and formulaic.

Humphry Repton, Brown's most important successor, defended the "Brunonian system" from many such complaints by asserting that the fault was often with inferior imitators. For example, writing in *An Enquiry into the Changes in Landscape Gardening* (1806) on the development in England of the naturalised landscape, he says:

> It was asserted, that nature must be our only model, and that nature abhorred a straight line: it was not therefore to be wondered at, that Brown's illiterate followers should have copied the means he used, and not the model he proposed: they saw him prefer curved lines to straight ones, and hence proceeded those meandering, serpentine, and undulating lines in all their works . . . Thus we see roads sweeping round, to avoid the direct line, to their object, and fences fancifully taking a longer course, and even belts and plantations in useless curves, with a drive meandering in parallel lines, which are full as much out of nature as a straight one.

The tone of this passage is typical of Repton in its respect for Brown which is tempered by common sense. So in his gardening practice he could sometimes produce results that recall Brown's work fairly closely, though he felt it impractical to do away invariably with formal garden terraces and he was not so concerned as Brown to hide the kitchen garden — not that Brown could be said to despise the kitchen garden. Repton also avoids one truly unnatural, though not always ineffective feature of the Brown landscape, a clump of trees isolated on the crest of a hill. Instead, as Dorothy Stroud puts it, "Repton's trees spilled like cream down the slopes to merge in the valleys". We are not, perhaps, in Repton's debt to the extent that we are in Brown's, who genuinely improved wide areas of land by proper drainage in what he called his "place making". But Repton paid more attention to everyday domestic life in his designs, he introduced greater variety and flexibility in planting and layout, he made important contributions to the history and theory of the subject, and the planting involved in Regency urban design drew much from him.

Repton's illustration of how to avoid, in tree planting, the dullness of a straight horizontal line at eye-level.

"The Genius"

Consult the Genius of the Place in all;
That tells the Waters or to rise, or fall;
Or helps th' ambitious hill the heav'ns to scale,
Or scoops in circling theatres the Vale;
Calls in the Country, catches op'ning glades,
Joins willing woods, and varies shades from shades;
Now breaks, or now directs, th' intending lines;
Paints as you plant, and, as you work, designs.

Still follow Sense, of ev'ry Art the Soul,
Parts answ'ring parts shall slide into a whole,
Spontaneous beauties all around advance,
Start ev'n from Difficulty, strike from Chance;
Nature shall join you; Time shall make it grow
A Work to wonder at — perhaps a STOWE.

Pope, *Epistle to Burlington.*

In this justly well-known passage on the principles of landscape gardening Pope inevitably elevates good sense above all else, advocating compromise and agreement with nature and accepting the principle of irregularity in the art. He suggests that when one has thus found the key to the appreciation of landscape, nature itself becomes animate and cooperative in a dreamlike and paradisal way that might be surprising to common sense, and "Spontaneous beauties all around advance". Pope wielded great influence upon eighteenth century landscape gardening not only through his literary works, for he was a keen gardener himself and expended much time, thought and money upon the creation of a poetic landscape at his Thames-side villa in Twickenham. As one might expect with the author of *The Rape of the Lock* he extracted a remarkable degree of variety from a very restricted space.

Maynard Mack in *The Garden and the City* (1969) has brilliantly demonstrated that when in the early 1720s Pope seemed ready to give up poetry and to live the squire's life gardening at Twickenham, he was far from being flippant, escapist or complacent. Rather, this retirement was intimately related to his progress as a poet, a necessary part of his creation of a persona fit for the writing of satire. Thus Pope's grotto at Twickenham, with its globular alabaster lamp, its *camera obscura* and its rugged walls studded with semi-precious stones, was in no sense a Folly. Indeed, we shall not be far wrong if we see Pope in this context as an almost Coleridgean figure of the poet retiring to the cave of creativity, or the unconscious, lighted by the lamp of imagination. Perhaps even more than his friend Lord Cobham, Pope was able to express the deepest springs of his being through his gardening, however urbane that activity might seem on the surface. "The Genius of the Place" was certainly no abstraction to Pope, and I think it was also rather more than just a Baroque pictorial adjunct of a kind familiar in Augustan poetry.

It was Pope who composed the verses for the Grotto at Henry Hoare's Stourhead, a pleasure-ground which is the perfect distillation of the eighteenth century feeling for an Arcady compounded of Virgil, Claude, and the man-of-taste's Grand Tour, during which he would hope to collect some Claude canvases as well as to contemplate the Ruins of Rome at first-hand. Kenneth Woodbridge has examined thoroughly the Virgilian association of the

Opposite above
Castle Howard, view from the South.

Opposite below
Castle Howard, the Temple of the Four Winds.

PLAN des Jardins de sa Grace le Duc de **BUCKINGHAM**,   A **PLAN** of the Gardens of His Grace the Duke of **BUCKINGHAM**,

A **STOWE.**   **AT STOWE.**

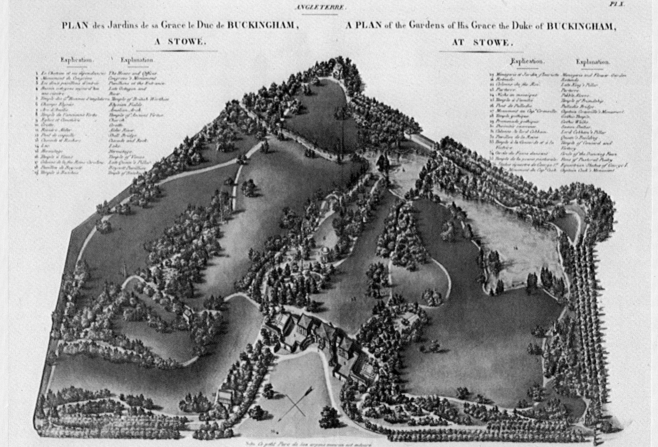

Explication.	Explanation.
1 Le Chateau et ses dépendances	The House and Offices
2 Monument de Congreve	Congreve's Monument
3 Les deux pavillons d'entrée	Pavillons at the Entrance
4 Bassin octogone auprès d'un rosarium	Lake Octagon and Rosa.
5 Temple des Hommes d'angleterre	Temple of British Worthies
6 Champs Elysées	Elysian Fields
7 Arc d'Anibe	Anubian Arch
8 Temple de l'ancienne Vertu	Temple of Ancient Virtue
9 Eglise et Cimetière	Church
10 Grotte	Grotto
11 Rivière r. Riller	Riller River
12 Pont de coquille	Shell Bridge
13 Chemin et Rocher	Channels and Rock
14 Lac	Lake
15 Hermitage	Hermitage
16 Temple de Vénus	Temple of Venus
17 Colonne de la Reine Caroline	Late Queen's Pillar
18 Pavillon de Boycott	Boycott Pavillions
19 Temple à Bacchus	Temple of Bacchus

Explication.	Explanation.
20 Ménagerie et Jardin d'fleuriste	Menagerie and Flower Garden
21 Rotonde	Rotunda
22 Colonne du feu Roi	Late King's Pillar
23 Parterre	Parterre
24 Niche en mosaïque	Pebble Alcove
25 Temple d'amitié	Temple of Friendship
26 Pont de Palladio	Palladio Bridge
27 Monument au Cap. Grenville	Captain Grenville's Monument
28 Temple gothique	Gothic Temple
29 Promenade gothique	Gothic Walks
30 Derstrtée saxonne	Saxon Deities
31 Colonne de Lord Cobham	Lord Cobham's Pillar
32 Pavillon de la Reine	Queen's Building
33 Temple à la Gloire et à la Victoire	Temple of Concord and Victory
34 Cercle des Fées dansant	Circle of the Dancing Fays
35 Temple de la poésie pastorale	Ruin of Pastoral Poetry
36 Statue équestre de George 1er	Equestrian Statue of George 1
37 Monument du Cap. Cook	Captain Cook's Monument

Nota. Ce petit Parc de dix arpens environ est entouré de tous côtés du Grand Parc d'environ six arpens.

Nota. This small Park of nearly ten Acres is surrounded on every side with the great one of nearly six Acres.

William Kent, *A Fantasy of Mr. Pope's Garden* (British Museum). Kent with his palette stands with his hands on Pope's shoulder on the right of the drawing.

Stourhead layout in *Landscape and Antiquity* (1970), and the passages from the *Aeneid* that he finds directly relevant to the garden represent moments of vision and divine revelation. For example, the relation between Stourhead and Claude's *Coast View of Delos with Aeneas* leads Woodbridge to quote Aeneas' account, from Virgil, of his experience in Apollo's Temple at Delos:

> . . . of a sudden everything seemed to quake, even the God's entrance-door and his bay-tree; the whole hill on which we stood appeared to move and the shrine seemed to open and the tripod within to speak with a roar. We bowed low and fell to the earth. A voice came to our ears: "O much enduring Dardans, the land of your ancestors whence you are sprung shall receive you on your return to her generous bosom. Seek out your ancient mother."

Similarly the passage associated with the Stourhead grotto, which Hoare meant to figure a descent into Avernus, has the landscape announcing by its agitation the coming of the god followed by the prophecy of finding a home.

Woodbridge concludes that Henry Hoare "was celebrating the founding of Rome, just as he, like Aeneas, was establishing his family in a place". This is no doubt true, but if we are to account properly for the artistic and psychological effects of the landscape we should be aware not just of the surface literary allusion, but also of the way in which the garden under

Opposite above
Wilton, the Palladian Bridge by Henry Herbert, 9th Earl of Pembroke. It was from this that the similar bridge at Stowe was imitated.

Opposite below
Stowe, Vergnaud's plan which gives to the grounds a Brown-like appearance.

Hoare's hand reproduces and manipulates the same archetypal patterns that lie behind the passages from the *Aeneid*. The grotto works a death and rebirth pattern in which one descends to contemplate the statue of the inspirational Nymph and then that of the fruitful River God prior to a rather more difficult ascent back to the surface. The whole garden, as the references to Virgil suggest, bespeaks the sacredness of the relation between man and animate nature; man rediscovers himself in terms of landscape and creates the sense of home, of belonging in nature. The imitation of a Claude picture is the pleasing surface of the garden, the *meaning* has to do with the recognition of the autonomy of landscape — and that it requires labour to produce a landscape garden, like any work of art, does not contradict this. The satyrs that people the woods at Rousham represent an attempt, using a pleasing but limited and sometimes archaic poetic vocabulary, to acknowledge the "Genius of the Place" as more than an abstraction or an escapist trifle. Capability Brown was not interested in the literary machinery that could be linked with landscape to express this process, but his grand and simple conception of the ideal landscape is an expression of the profound mood of reconciliation, renewal and unity that arises from Stourhead when properly viewed. When we learn to apprehend the Genius, when we respond to the archetypal level of meaning in the eighteenth century landscape garden, we can see how far the landscape movement was from being recreation in the sense of merely a rich man's playtime.

Selected Bibliography

Clark, H. F.	*The English Landscape Garden* (1948)
Clifford, Derek	*A History of Garden Design* (1962)
Gilpin, William	*Three Essays: On Picturesque Beauty; On Picturesque Travel; and On Sketching Landscape* (1792)
Green, David	*Gardener to Queen Anne* (1956)
Hadfield, Miles	*Gardening in Britain* (1960)
Hunt, John Dixon and Willis, Peter (eds.)	*The Genius of the Place: The English Landscape Garden, 1620-1820 (1975)*
Hussey, Christopher	*The Picturesque* (1927) *English Gardens and Landscapes 1700-1750* (1967)
Hyams, Edward	*The English Garden* (1972) *Capability Brown and Humphry Repton* (1971)
Jourdain, Margaret	*The Work of William Kent* (1948)
Knight, Richard P.	*The Landscape: A Didactic Poem* (1794)
Mack, Maynard	*The Garden and the City* (1969)
Malins, Edward	*English Landscaping and Literature 1660-1840* (1966)
Manwaring, Elizabeth	*Italian Landscape in Eighteenth Century England* (1925)
Parris, Leslie	*Landscape in Britain c.1750-1850* (1973)
Price, Uvedale	*An Essay on the Picturesque* (1794)
Repton, Humphry	*Observations on the Theory and Practice of Landscape Gardening* (1803) *An Enquiry into the Changes of Taste in Landscape Gardening* (1806)
Stroud, Dorothy	*Capability Brown* (1950) *Humphry Repton* (1962)
Vergnaud, N.	*L'Art de Créer les Jardins* (1839)
Walpole, Horace	"On Modern Gardening", *Anecdotes of Painting* (1770)
Woodbridge, Kenneth	*Landscape and Antiquity: Aspects of English Culture at Stourhead 1718-1838* (1970)

THE GARDENS

MELBOURNE HALL, DERBYSHIRE

The partnership of George London and Henry Wise laid out the garden for the Coke family at the end of the seventeenth and the beginning of the eighteenth centuries. Thomas Coke had chosen one of their plans "to suit with Versailles", as Wise put it. Coke himself was familiar with the work of André Le Nôtre who designed the gardens at Versailles; and, shortly before beginning plans for Melbourne, London toured French gardens for six months apparently meeting Le Nôtre in the process. The gently sloping garden was terraced and parterres were laid out in symmetrical geometric shapes, the whole being planted regularly with small evergreens and substantially hedged in clipped yew. Statuary, mainly by Jan Van Nost in the Dutch Baroque manner, plays an important part in the garden design. The sculptures take mainly heroic subjects, though there are also the four small pairs of cupids, probably by Van Nost, placed at intervals in the dark hedges. The sequence depicts a quarrel and reconciliation between the infant Castor and Pollux. At the far end of the large pond at Melbourne Hall stands a wrought-iron birdcage pergola of great charm and delicacy. It was created early in the eighteenth century by Robert Bakewell, a local blacksmith.

Above
The garden front of Melbourne Hall.

Right and opposite below
Quarrel and reconciliation, by Jan Van Nost.

Opposite above
Aerial view of Melbourne Hall, showing Wise's garden layout.

POWIS CASTLE, POWIS

Partly owing to the almost precipitous slope which they occupy, the seventeenth century formal terraced gardens at Powis survived the eighteenth century without being stripped according to the "Brunonian system". Not that they were admired in the eighteenth century in the way that they deserved, as Christopher Hussey indicates when he tells of Tennant's comments on his visit to the castle in 1781:

> He admitted that the views were good, but that was owing to the height at which the Castle is perched, as a result of which you "experience the horrible vicissitudes of cold and heat", and "the gardens are to be descended to by terraces below terraces, a laborious flight of steps". The gardens as a whole he found "in wretched taste".

The terraces do indeed offer a magnificent prospect over the Severn valley, and this, together with the fact that what were once small, neat, clipped hedges have now grown greatly, prevents the tedium that is sometimes associated with formality in garden design.

Humphry Repton might almost be describing Powis when he says in his *Enquiry:* "The Italian style of gardens consisted in balustraded terraces of masonry, magnificent flights of steps, arcades, and architectural grottoes, lofty clipped hedges, with niches and recesses enriched by sculpture". These are the features which gradually disappeared from the ideal naturalised landscape of the eighteenth century, which tends to look more like the surrounding countryside overlooked by Powis than the castle gardens themselves.

Above
Pastoral sculpture and urns decorate the balustrades of terraced gardens at Powis.

Opposite above
Powis Castle.

Opposite below
Powis, the terraced garden.

Pages 26-27
View from the terrace at Powis.

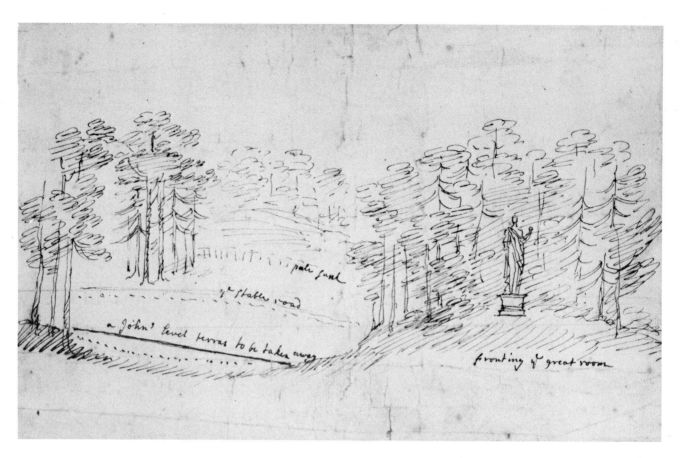

Top
Drawing by William Kent for the view "fronting ye great room" at Claremont, Surrey. Kent's note "a Johns level terras to be taken away" refers to Sir John Vanbrugh's terrace. (British Museum)

Above
Kent's drawing for the view towards the Belvedere at Claremont. Here Kent can be seen using the technique of clump-planting, of which Walpole complained: "His clumps were puny, he aimed at immediate effect, and planted not for futurity." (British Museum)

CASTLE HOWARD, YORKSHIRE

The view from the South shows the grand manner and sublime scale of the scene at Castle Howard, created mainly by Sir John Vanbrugh and Nicholas Hawksmoor who started work here in 1699. Their landscape design equals the later achievements of Capability Brown's gardens and there is a boldness in their architectural and landscape work at Castle Howard which makes the Palladian ideals of the Burlington circle, which came to dominate English taste early in the eighteenth century, seem rather tame.

The Temple of the Four Winds was designed by Vanbrugh between 1724 and 1726 and is a masterpiece of landscape building which, with Hawksmoor's Mausoleum, Sacheverell Sitwell claimed to be a greater work of art "than many of our cathedrals".

Hawksmoor's Mausoleum, designed 1728 to 1729, has been described by Christopher Hussey as "one of the master type-buildings of English architecture" and Horace Walpole thought it so fine that it "would tempt one to be buried alive". Lord Carlisle intended that he and his line should be entombed there, hence its climactic prominence in this heroic landscape design. Though it is no doubt correct to say that Lord Carlisle's aim at Castle Howard was to create a Virgilian Elysium, Hawksmoor's Mausoleum in its Yorkshire setting creates an atmosphere of noble melancholy that belongs as much to the Gothic North as to the Classical South.

Above
Castle Howard, the Mausoleum.

ROUSHAM, OXFORDSHIRE

This is the best surviving garden by William Kent, who here worked over an earlier layout by Charles Bridgeman. It may also be that Pope had a hand in the garden. Kent began his improvements at Rousham in the early 1730s and, Christopher Hussey suggests, Bridgeman may have continued on the site carrying out "the more technical parts" of Kent's plans. This garden probably justifies Walpole's high praise of Kent, for it is a skilful painterly composition which can still be experienced by following the circuit which Kent intended. One passes the statue of the Dying Gladiator situated at the top of the Praeneste, a classical arcade not encountered until later in the circuit. The Praeneste terrace offers a view over the serpentine Cherwell and, in the opposite direction, of Kent's castellated lodge and Palladian doorway, flanked by white marble statues. Venus' Vale, using ponds and a picturesque cascade, no doubt owes something to the overgrown grottoes Kent would have seen in Italian gardens. From "Townsend's Temple", designed by Kent and built by William Townsend of Oxford, is a vista into which Heyford Bridge is drawn as

a picturesque element. Further upstream Kent converted an old mill, visible from the garden at Rousham, into the Temple of the Mill by adding an arched and pinnacled superstructure to one side of the house. A mile or so beyond the Temple of the Mill Kent echoed his construction by erecting his "eyecatcher", an arched façade intended simply to add picturesque interest to the skyline.

Of Kent's best work, like that at Rousham, Walpole wrote:

The gentle stream was taught to serpentize . . . Its borders were smoothed, but preserved their waving irregularity. A few trees scattered here and there on its edges sprinkled the tame bank that accompanied its meanders; and when it disappeared among the hills, shades descending from the heights leaned towards its progress, and framed the distant point of light under which it was lost, as it turned aside to either hand of the blue horizon.
Thus dealing in none but the colours of nature, men saw a new creation opening before their eyes. The living landscape was chastened or polished, not transformed.

Above
Venus' Vale at Rousham, showing the statue of Pan by Jan Van Nost.

Top
William Kent's eye-catcher from behind. Rousham House can
be seen in the distance through the central arch.

Above
Skyline with the eye-catcher.

Opposite
The Temple of the Mill across the Cherwell.

Above
Townsend's Temple.

Above
The Cascade, Venus' Vale.

Left
Cupid and Swan, Venus' Vale.

Opposite above
Kent's eye-catcher.

Opposite below
Venus' Vale, where the statue is an imitation of the Venus de Medici.

Page 36
Venus' Vale, another view.

Page 37, top
The Palladian doorway.

Page 37, below left
The memorial to the otter-hound is a playful touch comparable to the tablet to Signor Fido at Stowe.

Page 37, below right
Kent's marble figures flanking the Palladian doorway.

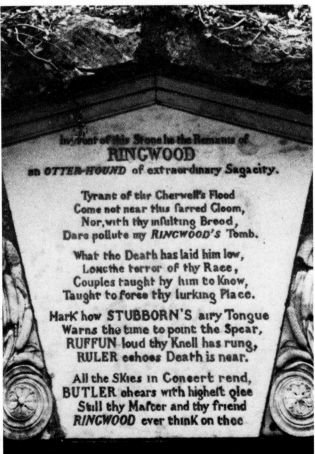

In front of this Stone lie the Remains of
RINGWOOD
an *OTTER-HOUND* of extraordinary Sagacity.

Tyrant of the Cherwell's Flood
Come not near this sarred Gloom,
Nor, with thy insulting Brood,
Dare pollute my *RINGWOOD'S* Tomb.

What tho Death has laid him low,
Lonc the terror of thy Race,
Couples taught by him to Know,
Taught to force thy lurking Place.

Mark how **STUBBORN'S** airy Tongue
Warns the time to point the Spear,
RUFFUN loud thy Knell has rung,
RULER echoes Death is near.

All the Skies in Consert rend,
BUTLER ohears with highest glee
Still thy Master and thy friend
RINGWOOD ever think on thee

A Faun, by Jan van Nost.

Pan, by Jan van Nost.

Top
Kent's castellated lodge at Rousham. The haha leading up to it
is here considerably overgrown.

Above
The Dying Gladiator, Praeneste terrace.

Opposite
Bacchus, by Jan Van Nost.

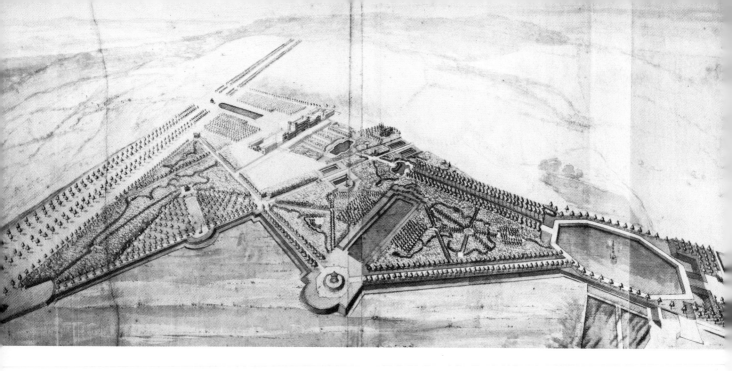

STOWE, BUCKINGHAMSHIRE

The various phases of development of the grounds at Stowe in the eighteenth century can be seen in the plans reproduced here. First there is Charles Bridgeman's perspective drawing of 1722-3, showing such regular features as the Octagon Lake to the south of the house, though many serpentine lines are also in evidence. The outline of the lake had been naturalised under Kent's aegis in the 1730s, as shown in J. Miller's plan of 1769. Finally, N. Vergnaud's nineteenth century plan of Stowe probably shows the grounds conforming rather more to

Capability Brown's manner than they ever did in fact, for Vergnaud was heavily committed to the Brown ideal landscape.

Above
Charles Bridgeman's perspective drawing of Stowe.

Below
Temple of Ancient Virtue, with Stowe church in the background where Capability Brown was married.

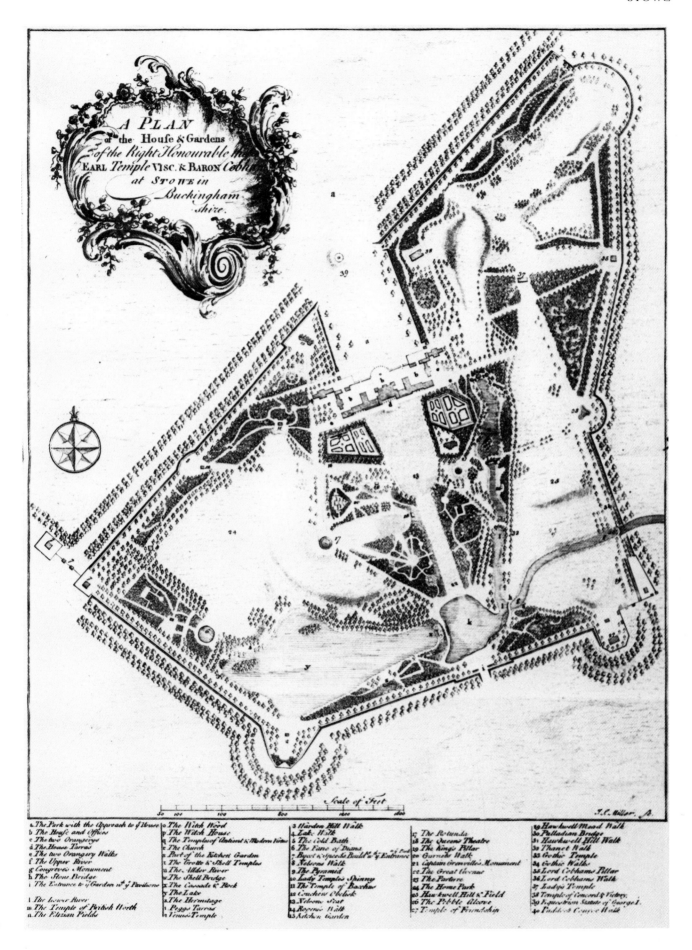

J. Miller's plan of Stowe: the manner of Kent.

The south vista at Stowe from across the Octagon Lake.

The south vista at Stowe by N. Vergnaud.

The Monument to Congreve, by Sir John Vanbrugh.

Opposite above
Kent's drawing for the Temple of Ancient Virtue at Stowe. The building faces the Monument to the British Worthies across Kent's version of the river Styx, now called the Worthies River. In the eighteenth century a heap of ruins stood nearby — Cobham's comment on Modern Virtue! (British Museum)

Opposite below
Temple of Ancient Virtue, an eighteenth century engraving.

Left
Temple of Ancient Virtue across the "Styx".

Below
William Kent's Monument to the British Worthies at Stowe, celebrating great Englishmen in the worlds of statecraft, commerce and the arts. Cobham's Whig principles are reflected in the men included here, like John Hampden and William III. A niche was also reserved for Alexander Pope for whom Stowe was a model of good taste in garden design. At the back of the Monument there used to be a facetious memorial inscription to one of Cobham's favourite greyhounds, "Signor Fido, an *Italian* of good Extraction; who came into *England*, not to bite us, like most of his Countrymen, but to gain an honest Livelihood".

Above and below

The Palladian Bridge at Stowe, designed by James Gibbs. This was imitated from Lord Pembroke's bridge at Wilton (1737), which in turn was inspired by Palladio's design for the Rialto Bridge in Venice. Because the bridge at Stowe had to allow for carriage traffic it was not possible to elevate it in the graceful manner of the Wilton bridge. Originally the farther side of the Stowe bridge did not have an open colonnade, for what lay beyond was not considered fit to be part of the garden's design. Somewhat in the manner of the false bridge at Kenwood the profile of Stowe's Palladian bridge completed the picture of the river which had been created on the inner side only.

Opposite, above left

Lord Cobham's memorial pillar, designed by James Gibbs. The pillar still stands, but without the statue of Cobham at the top.

Opposite, above right

The Pebble Alcove. "It is a little Grot, neatly adorned with Pebbles", says the eighteenth century guide-book. "His Lordship's Arms are curiously wrought upon the Back-wall with the same Materials, and displayed in different Colours, which has a very pretty and agreeable Effect".

Opposite, below

"How beautiful are thy temples" — a pun, in the Pebble Alcove, on the Cobham family name of Temple.

Above
The Gothic Temple or Temple of Liberty at Stowe. Even early in the eighteenth century the Gothic style was valued, particularly by Whigs, because it was associated with the British love of liberty. This strange three-sided building is not much like an authentic medieval building, though in the eighteenth century most would have agreed that "It is impossible to make a better Imitation of the ancient Taste of Architecture".

Left
Bust of William III in the Monument of British Worthies. William was generally regarded in the early eighteenth century as the upholder of British constitutional freedom who saved England from absolute monarchy of the kind which existed in France.

One of the Pavilions at the Entrance.

The Shepherds Cove.

An Artificial Piece of Ruins.

Above and Page 52, top
Some of the features of eighteenth century Stowe, including
the Shepherd's Cove or Hermitage.

The Temple dedicated to Venus.

The Hermitage. Eighteenth century gardens often cultivated a sense of retirement and moods of contemplation. The grounds at Stowe also included St. Augustine's Cave, the Sleeping-Parlour, the Temple of Contemplation, and the Grotto. One eighteenth century nobleman even went so far as to hire a hermit to occupy the hermitage which he built in his grounds, but he was ultimately unable to find anyone who could comply with the seven-year contract he stipulated.

Opposite
Studley Royal, the lower lake seen from the Gothic tower overlooking the gardens on the east side of the valley.

STUDLEY ROYAL, YORKSHIRE

The impressive water-gardens at Studley Royal were laid out for John Aislabie in the 1720s. The landscape design involves straight-sided canals and the circular and crescent Moon Ponds flanked by Classical temples and groups of Carpenter's statuary. William Aislabie, John's son, later acquired the upper part of the Skell valley which included the Gothic ruins of Fountains Abbey. These ruins became the focal point of the more naturalised landscape in this part of the valley.

Opposite
Studley Royal, part of the Moon Ponds layout, with Roman wrestlers by Carpenter seen from the Gothic tower.

Above
Studley Royal, a corner of the ponds.

STOURHEAD, WILTSHIRE

Henry Hoare was known in his family as Henry the Magnificent, which is not surprising in the light of his achievement at Stourhead. He began to create his Claudian landscape here in the 1740s, and it remains one of the loveliest and most important of eighteenth century landscape gardens, even though further planting of flowering shrubs in the nineteenth century was not part of the original scheme. It has been suggested that the eighteenth century landscape gardener's lack of concern for flowers was a result of his being inspired primarily by landscape paintings.

Hoare formed a lake in the valley at Stourhead and round it a walk that provides visitors with a sequence of picturesque views — as well, perhaps, as a celebration of the founding of Rome and of the founding of Hoare's own family at Stourhead. He employed as architect Henry Flitcroft, who like Kent was a protégé of Lord Burlington. Flitcroft designed most of the classical buildings that enrich the composition; the Temple of Flora, the Temple of Apollo, adapted from the Temple of Venus at Baalbec, and the deservedly renowned Pantheon, probably based as much upon the comparable building in Claude's painting *Aeneas at Delos* as upon the Roman original.

The Stourhead circuit takes the visitor into a grotto, affording a picturesquely framed view back across the lake and containing two sculptures by John Cheere; one is of the River God, and the other of the Sleeping Nymph, for which Pope, translating Bembo, wrote the following lines:

> Nymph of the Grot these sacred springs I keep
> And to the murmur of these waters sleep;
> Ah! spare my slumbers, gently tread the cave,
> And drink in silence or in silence lave.

> . . . your great Artist, like the source of light,
> Gilds every scene with beauty and delight;
> At Blenheim, Croome, and Caversham we trace
> Salvator's Wildness, Claud's enlivening grace,
> Cascades and Lakes as fine as Risdale drew,
> While Nature's vary'd in each charming view.

> He barren tracts with every charm illumes,
> At his command a new Creation blooms;
> Born to grace Nature, and her works complete,
> With all that's beautiful, sublime and great!
> For him each Muse enwreathes the Lawrel Crown,
> And consecrates to Fame immortal Brown.
> Anon., *The Rise and Progress of the Present Taste in Planting* (1767)

Opposite
View from the grotto at Stourhead showing the parish church, the bridge taken from a design by Palladio, and the Bristol Cross, a medieval Gothic market-cross erected near the entrance of the grounds in 1768.

Top
J. M. Turner, *At Stourhead*. Watercolour, *c*. 1800.

Above
J. M. Turner, *The Bristol Cross, Stourhead*. Watercolour, *c*. 1800.

Flitcroft's Temple of Apollo

Flitcroft's Pantheon

The Stourhead Lake, with Flitcroft's Temple of Flora. The dome of the Temple of Apollo can be seen among the trees on the hillside, and the urn marks one of the springs of the lake.

Above

Alfred's Tower. Flitcroft designed this three-sided tower, erected on Kingsnettle Hill some distance from the pleasure ground. On this hill King Alfred was reputed to have raised his standard in A.D. 870 in the struggle against the Danes. In its reference to contemporary events — it celebrated the peace with Spain concluded in 1762 — and in its representation of an enlightened ideal of kingship the "sublime" Alfred's Tower recalls Lord Cobham's Stowe.

The Bristol Cross.

Alfred's Tower, statue and inscription. The inscription reads:

Alfred's Tower.

ALFRED THE GREAT
A.D. 870 on this Summit
Erected his Standard
Against Danish Invaders
To him We owe the origin of Juries
The Establishment of a Militia
The Creation of a Naval Force
ALFRED The Light of a Benighted Age
Was a Philosopher and a Christian
The Father of His People
The Founder of the English
MONARCHY and LIBERTY

Top
Francis Nicholson, *Temple of Flora, Stourhead*. Watercolour,
1813.

Above
Francis Nicholson, *The Grotto, Stourhead*. Watercolour, 1813.

Top
Francis Nicholson, *The Pantheon and Gothic Watch-Cottage, Stourhead*. Watercolour, 1813. The Gothic cottage was not erected until early in the nineteenth century.

Above
Francis Nicholson, *Lake and Cascade, Stourhead*. Watercolour, 1813.

LANCELOT "CAPABILITY" BROWN

Lancelot "Capability" Brown.

Bards yet unborn
Shall pay to Brown, that tribute fitliest paid
In strains the beauty of his scenes inspire.

William Mason, *The English Garden* (1772)

LANCELOT "CAPABILITY" BROWN
(1716–1783)

Thomas Hughes was probably not thinking of Capability Brown, but his words have a particular application to the great gardener when he writes in *Tom Brown's Schooldays:* "much has yet to be written and said before the British nation will be properly sensible of how much of its greatness it owes to the Browns. For centuries, in their quiet, dogged, homespun way, they have been subduing the earth in most English counties." The note sounded in the word "subduing" may be a little too militantly Victorian, but even admirers of Brown acknowledged that he took a firm hand with nature. For example, William Whitehead causes Brown to address Nature itself thus, in *The Late Improvements at Nuneham* (1787):

Observe all these changes, and candidly own
I have cloath'd you when naked, and when o'erdrest
I have stripped you again to your boddice and vest.

A newspaper obituary said of Brown at his death in 1783:

His great and fine genius stood unrivalled, and it was the peculiar felicity of it that it was allowed by all ranks and degrees of society in this country, and by many noble and great personages in other countries. Those who knew him best, or practised near him were not able to determine whether the quickness of his eye or its correctness, were most to be admired. It was comprehensive and elegant, and perhaps it may be said never to have failed him. Such, however, was the effect of his genius that when he was the happiest man, he will be least remembered; so closely did he copy nature that his works will be mistaken.

Above
Brown's landscape at Petworth, West Sussex, showing clump-planting.

HAREWOOD, YORKSHIRE

The long and ample stretch of water that Brown created here is characteristic of his style. He was responsible for much of the planting at Harewood although the lakeside rhododendrons are, like those at Stourhead, a later addition to the eighteenth century design.

Above
Aerial view of Harewood.

BLENHEIM, OXFORDSHIRE

Blenheim Palace was designed by Vanbrugh as a gift from the nation to the Duke of Marlborough in gratitude for his victory in the Battle of Blenheim (1704). Capability Brown began work on the grounds early in the 1760s. His designs took ten years to execute at a cost of £30,000. Characteristically he broke up the formality of the park, sweeping away the formal parterres by Henry Wise and taking smooth turf up to the palace itself. The aerial view of Blenheim shows that some elements of geometric French garden design have been reintroduced on the east and west sides of the house. One of Brown's greatest triumphs was his creation of the twin lakes at Blenheim which match the grandiose scale of Vanbrugh's bridge. In Vanbrugh's design the bridge spanned a diminutive and canalised River Glyme —

which is not to say that Vanbrugh simply made an error of judgement here, as it has often been represented. In his day the main approach to the palace lay over the bridge, so that its profile was not so important, and no doubt Vanbrugh felt that the modesty of the stream served to emphasise the grandeur of the bridge. It is supposed to have been his transformation of Vanbrugh's lakes at Blenheim that caused Capability Brown to remark: "Thames, Thames, you will never forgive me!"

Above
Blenheim Palace from the north-west.

Below
The bridge at Blenheim seen from a lakeside clump of trees.

Top
Vergnaud's plan of Brown's layout at Blenheim (1839). This illustrates well Brown's use of the irregular belt of trees to surround the park and shows how he broke the long avenue of trees approaching the palace from the north-west into clumps.

Above
Blenheim Palace, an aerial view from the south. Much clump-planting remains, but the great avenue of trees has reappeared.

Opposite
Harewood, Capability Brown's lake.

Opposite above
Harewood, the landscape park. The striking beauty of Brown's park is seen from the formal terrace, added after he had finished work here.

Opposite below
Harewood, the cascade by which the water flows from Brown's lake.

Above
Looking eastward across the Blenheim lake toward Woodstock.

Top
Vergnaud's somewhat romanticised nineteenth century view of Blenheim across the lake. The artist has almost transformed Vanbrugh's Baroque palace into a castle of medieval romance.

Above
Vanbrugh's bridge over Brown's lake at Blenheim.

Left
A row of trees on the west side of the great avenue.

Opposite left
The Column of Victory at Blenheim. A statue of Marlborough, like a heroic Roman, stands at the top. The column stands in the avenue that leads across the bridge from the palace.

Opposite right
The Column of Victory from behind. The palace and the road leading from the bridge can be seen in the distance.

CASTLE ASHBY, NORTHAMPTONSHIRE

Brown undertook to remodel the grounds here for the Earl of Northampton in 1761. Castle Ashby formerly had long avenues of trees radiating north, south, west and east from the house — the kind of arrangement to which Humphry Repton rationally objected that it made all vistas the same. Brown dispensed with the north and west avenues, kept the south, and broke up the east into clumps. He was not, however, a wanton destroyer of trees as some of his detractors claimed, for he must have planted immeasurably more than he uprooted. At Castle Ashby he planted a considerable number of trees, as well as converting a number of small ponds into two large lakes. He designed the Gothic Menagerie which can be seen from the house across the lake to which it gives its name.

Above
The formal gardens at Castle Ashby. Its urns, terraces and dark clipped hedges contrast markedly with Brown's naturalised landscape beyond.

Below
View towards the upper lake. The ground at the right of the picture slopes down to form a haha.

Brown's Menagerie at Castle Ashby.

Overleaf
View across the formal garden to Brown's landscape. The
Menagerie can be seen in the top right-hand corner.

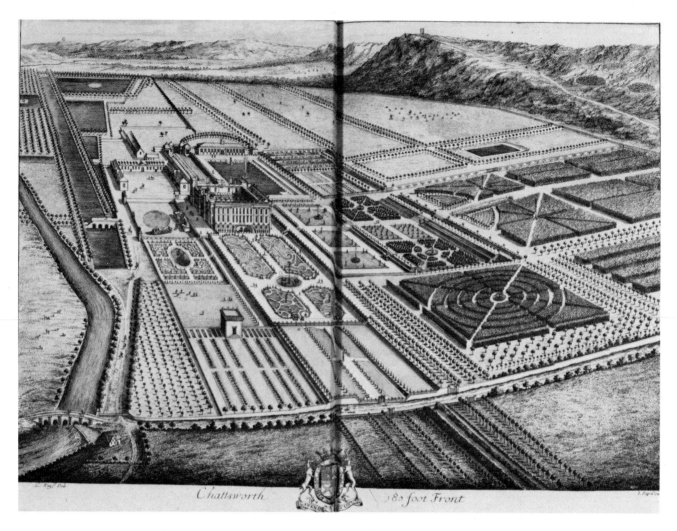

Chattsworth   180 foot Front

CHATSWORTH, DERBYSHIRE

Writing early in the nineteenth century in his *Beauties of England and Wales* John Britton had this to say about the Great Cascade which was a striking feature of George London's formal garden begun at Chatsworth in 1688:

The *Water-Works,* which, fifty or sixty years ago, gave the gardens of Chatsworth a celebrity that they have not yet lost, are situated near the south-east and south sides of the house. Though still in tolerable order, they fail to interest, as the improved taste of the present day can only regard them as formal puerilities. The principal of these artificial contrivances is the great Cascade, which consists of a series of steps or stages, extending a considerable distance down a steep hill, crowned at the top by a temple, which is supplied with water from a reservoir, which occupies several acres. "This fane," observes Mr. Warner, "should certainly be dedicated to Mercury, the god of fraud and deceit, as a piece of roguery is practised upon the incautious stranger within its very sanctuary; from the floor of which a multitude of little fountains suddenly spout up whilst he is admiring

the prospect through the portal, and quickly wet him to the skin."

This tone, bantering and dismissive, is typical of the latter half of the eighteenth century, for, as Walpole said in 1770, "Fountains have with great reason been banished from gardens as unnatural".

To Charles Cotton, writing in the latter half of the seventeenth century, the formality of the gardens at Chatsworth was like paradise, in striking contrast to what seemed to him the shameful untidiness of Nature in the surrounding Derbyshire countryside:

The *Groves,* whose curled *Brows* shade ev'ry *Lake*
Do ev'rywhere such waving *Landskips* make,
As *Painter's* baffled *Art* is far above,
Who *Waves* and *Leaves* could never yet make
   move . . .
To view from hence the glitt'ring Pile above . . .
Environ'd round with Nature's Shames and Ills,

Above
Chatsworth in the seventeenth century, from Kip's *Views*.

Chatsworth after Brown's alterations, a nineteenth century engraving.

Black Heath, Wild Rock, bleak Craggs, and naked
  Hills,
Who is it, but must presently conclude,
That this is *Paradise;* which seated stands
In midst of Deserts, and of barren *Sands?*

Cotton is obviously close to Thomas Burnet's theory, outlined in his *Theory of the Earth* (1684-90), that it was part of the misfortune of fallen man to inherit a fallen, ruined, and chaotic Nature. The "wild, vast and undigested heaps of stones and earth", as Burnet characterized the Swiss Alps, were taken as evidence of a ruined earth, a corner of which seventeenth century Chatsworth was an attempt to repair. Eighteenth century Chatsworth outgrew the idea that paradise was to be regained by imposing geometrical patterns upon nature.

By the time that Chatsworth had passed to the fourth Duke of Devonshire the reaction against the London and Wise concept of the garden was well established. The Duke invited Capability Brown to remodel the grounds, which he began to do in 1760. Brown undertook a great deal of tree-planting both on the house side of the river Derwent, once a bare hillside, and on the village side which today still preserves the features of a Brown landscape. He widened, smoothed and raised the river by constructing a weir and laid a gentle slope of turf between house and water. He did not, however, do away with the Great Cascade, though he replaced the formal flower-beds that had flanked it with lawns.

The nineteenth century saw a return to formality evident in some parts of the garden layout at Chatsworth. Between 1836 and 1839 Joseph Paxton built the Great Conservatory here, an impressive iron-and-glass construction that was a prototype of his Crystal Palace made for the Great Exhibition of 1851. The Conservatory, like the Palace, has since disappeared, though its site is marked by a maze. Paxton was also responsible for the powerful Emperor Fountain, set in the Canal Pond which dates from the early years of the eighteenth century. The other fountain on the south side of the house, the Seahorse Fountain, was part of the seventeenth century layout.

Top
A picturesque nineteenth century rendering of Chatsworth
from Brown's weir.

Above
View over Chatsworth from the hillside which in Kip's
seventeenth century engraving is shown with very few trees.

Opposite
Chatsworth seen from across the Derwent, whose water has
the placid appearance so favoured by Brown.

Top
The Great Cascade in the eighteenth century.

Above
The Great Cascade now.

Top
View over Brown's landscape from the side of the Canal Pond.

Above
Brown's park at Chatsworth, looking north.

Above and opposite
The Temple at the head of the Great Cascade.

Above
The Hermitage at Chatsworth.

Opposite, top
The south front at Chatsworth, showing the seventeenth century Seahorse Fountain.

Opposite, centre
South front, looking along the Canal Pond from which springs the 290 foot jet of Paxton's Emperor Fountain.

Opposite, bottom
The maze which marks the site of Paxton's Great Conservatory at Chatsworth.

BURGHLEY, NORTHAMPTONSHIRE

More than a quarter of a century was spent in the execution of Brown's designs at Burghley, where his work was commissioned in the 1750s. Naturally he removed the old formal garden, though one long avenue of trees remains. He created an impressive thirty-two acre lake and the Lion Bridge which crosses it and reshaped and replanted the large park. Dorothy Stroud quotes a letter written by Lord Dacre in 1756 in which there is the following reference to Brown's employment at Burghley: "He tells me that he has the alteration of Burghleigh and that not only of the Park but of the House which wherever it is Gothick he intends to preserve in that stile: and whatever new ornaments he adds are to be so." Both the stables and the orangery designed by Brown for Burghley are in the "Gothick stile".

Above
Brown's Lion Bridge at Burghley.

Left
Burghley House, from the haha which disguises the distinction between garden and park.

Opposite above
One of the four lions which gave the Lion Bridge its name.

Opposite below
Brown's Gothick Orangery at Burghley.

BUCKINGHAM PALACE, LONDON

An aerial view over Buckingham Palace, which is not generally associated with the naturalised ideal of landscape of the eighteenth century. But Nikolaus Pevsner observes in *The Englishness of English Art:* "The façade known to Londoners is . . . an early twentieth century addition by Sir Aston Webb and with the *rond-point* in front of it more Parisian than Londonian in spirit. The real front of the Palace faces west, that is faces a spacious lawn, winding paths, and a serpentine lake with an island."

KEW, LONDON

In the busy decade of the 1760s Brown was employed at the Royal Park at Richmond, adjoining Kew Gardens with which it was merged by George III after the death of Queen Caroline. Thus Brown's park has become one with that of his rival and detractor Sir William Chambers. Chambers attempted to introduce into England his bizarre version of the Chinese taste in gardening, and his Pagoda at Kew is a relic of this. He was also responsible for the Temple of Bellona and the Ruined Arch which was intended to impart something of the romance of the *Campagna* to Kew.

In the Royal Park Brown did away with the formal garden of Queen Caroline, destroying Merlin's Cave designed by the Queen's protégé Stephen Duck, the peasant poet. Brown also scooped out the rhododendron dell at Kew, employing a company of soldiers for the operation. He made the lake and landscaped the ground by the Thames, across which there is a view of Syon House where Brown was also employed. Brown was much respected by George III who was even somewhat in awe of his head-gardener. When Brown died George is reported to have said to one of the other royal gardeners: "Mellicant, I hear that Brown is dead. Now you and I can do as we please."

Above
The Ruined Arch at Kew.

The Temple of Bellona, Kew.

The Temple of Aeolus, Kew.

Sir William Chamber's Chinese Pagoda at Kew.

Opposite
Kew, the Temple of Aeolus.

Sir William Chambers, in *A Dissertation on Oriental Gardening* (1772), wrote of Capability Brown's style of landscape gardening:

> At his first entrance [into a park by Brown], the stranger is treated with the sight of a large green field, scattered over with a few straggling trees, and verged with a confused border of little shrubs and flowers: upon further inspection he finds a little serpentine path, twining in regular *esses,* amongst the shrubs of the border: upon which he is to go round to look on one side at the boundary, which is never more than a few yards from him, and always obtruding upon his sight: from time to time he perceives a little seat or temple stuck up against the wall; he rejoices at the discovery, sits down, rests his wearied limbs, and then reels on again, cursing the line of beauty; till spent with fatigue, half-roasted by the sun, (for there is never any shade), and tired for want of entertainment, he resolves to see no more — vain resolution! there is but one path; he must either drag on to the end, or return back by the tedious way he came.
>
> Such is the favourite plan of our smaller gardens: and our larger works are only a repetition of the smaller ones; like the honest bachelor's feast, which consisted in nothing but a multiplication of his own dinner — three legs of mutton, three roasted geese, and three buttered apple-pies.

Above
The Lily Pond, Kew.

Page 98
Syon, the lake constructed by Brown.

Page 99
Kew, a view across Brown's lake showing Syon House where Brown was also employed.

Opposite
Kew, the Rhododendron Dell, for which Brown was responsible. He was able to avail himself of a company of George III's soldiers to dig the valley from a flat site.

SYON, LONDON

While Robert Adam was employed at Syon to remodel the house, Brown worked over the gardens, finishing in 1773. The long and narrow lake that Brown made at Syon remains a feature of great beauty, and much of his rich and varied tree-planting is also still in evidence. However, many changes have taken place in the two hundred years since Brown's alterations. Among the most interesting is the Great Conservatory designed by Charles Fowler and executed in the 1820s. It provided the inspiration for Paxton's greenhouses at Chatsworth, which in turn led to the monumental Crystal Palace.

Opposite above
Syon House, view across the Thames from Kew.

Above
A peacock among Brown's lakeside planting at Syon.

Opposite below
Charles Fowler's Great Conservatory at Syon. The urns in
front are by Grinling Gibbons.

DODINGTON, GLOUCESTERSHIRE

The present house at Dodington, designed by James Wyatt, was built more than thirty years after Brown began reshaping the surrounding landscape in 1764. Much of Brown's park, however, remains intact. There are, for example, his two lakes which are on different levels and connected by a striking Gothic cascade. The contours of the Cotswold valley suited Brown's style and he opened the landscape here by removing trees where necessary.

Brown wrote expressively of the effect of his work at Dodington: "All obdurate lines softened into curves, the terrace melted into a swelling bank and the walks opened to catch the vicinal country".

Above
View across the lower lake at Dodington, showing the east front of the house.

Left
At the north-east edge of the lower lake.

Right
Brown's Gothic Cascade at Dodington. Behind is Wyatt's Church of St. Mary, joined by the conservatory to the house itself.

HOLKHAM, NORFOLK

The grandiose and severe mansion at Holkham was designed by William Kent. Brown worked over the grounds in the early 1760s and Repton prepared a Red Book for Holkham in 1789. In the nineteenth century the gardens were further substantially altered. However, many features of Brown's work are still evident at Holkham. He set the house in a wide expanse of grass, screening the kitchen gardens with trees and employing the characteristic smooth surfaces of water and clump-planting. Brown would surely have been appalled by the nineteenth century formal terrace with its fountains.

Kent was responsible for the Obelisk, commemorating the beginning of the planting of the park in 1729 and the temple in the Obelisk Wood.

Above
The south front of Holkham seen between examples of clump-planting.

Below left
Holkham from the south-west across the lake.

Below right
Kent's Temple in the Obelisk Wood.

View south into the park at Holkham across the nineteenth century Perseus and Andromeda fountain. Kent's Obelisk can be seen on the skyline.

Above
The Andromeda fountain and the park.

Below
The park south of the house.

TEMPLE NEWSAM, YORKSHIRE

The extreme simplicity of design — the clumps of trees, the shorn turf extending right up to the house — show why exponents of the Picturesque school could complain of the baldness of Brown's style.

Opposite above
Temple Newsam, the house and park.

Opposite below
Temple Newsam, a good example of the kind of clump-planting employed by Brown who took these grounds in hand in 1765.

WESTON PARK, SHROPSHIRE

Brown was called in to landscape Weston Park some time after Sir Henry Bridgeman succeeded to the property in 1762. He worked closely with James Paine who designed the exquisite Temple of Diana, round which Brown formed the Temple Wood. Paine also created the Roman Bridge and "little temple" that face each other across the Temple Pool. The urns in Brown's wood are probably by Paine as well. Great sweeps of lawn, clumps of trees, a wide serpentine lake and impressive vistas to the surrounding hills all mark this as a representative Capability Brown landscape, despite the formal terraced gardens added near the house during the nineteenth century.

Above
View towards the east front of the house at Weston from the steps of Paine's Temple of Diana.

The Temple of Diana by James Paine. The sunken stone wall
of the haha can be seen in the foreground of this picture.

Opposite
Newby Hall, a mossy statue of Bacchus in an atmospheric and
reflective avenue of statuary with classical subjects in the
eighteenth century gardens.

A nineteenth century engraving showing Weston Hall from the
south-east.

Overleaf
Paine's "little temple" by the Temple Pool.

Paine's Roman Bridge at Weston.

Top
View towards the east front at Weston across Brown's park.

Above
Brown's clump-planting at Weston.

KENWOOD, HAMPSTEAD

In 1754 William Murray, later the first Earl of Masefield, bought Kenwood House which, a little over ten years later, he engaged Robert Adam to alter. The Earl saw to the remodelling of his park and it is recorded that he planted the cedars here with his own hands. One of the most striking features of the grounds is the false bridge set at one end of the lake to improve the prospect by giving the impression that the lake flows on into a river. In this respect it recalls the Palladian bridge at Stowe.

Above
Kenwood across the lake.

Opposite above
The profile of the dummy bridge at Kenwood.

Opposite below
The Kenwood bridge revealed as façade only!

LONGLEAT, WILTSHIRE

A visitor to Longleat in 1760 wrote: "We got to Longleat! There is not much alteration in the house *but the gardens are no more!* They are succeeded by a fine lawn, a serpentine river, wooded hills, gravel paths meandering round a shrubbery, *all modernised* by the ingenious and much sought after *Mr. Brown*!" Repton also did some work at Longleat in 1803, though the landscape remains primarily Brown's. The view from "Heaven's Gate", shown here is probably the most impressive surviving vista of an eighteenth century landscape garden.

Above
The view from "Heavens Gate" over Longleat as it was in the nineteenth century.

Below
The same view today.

ST. JOHN'S COLLEGE, CAMBRIDGE

Brown planned the alterations to the grounds of St. John's College in 1772. The work came about through his friendship with John Mainwaring, Professor of Theology and fellow of the College. At St. John's Brown created the Wilderness, or Fellows' Garden, out of a bowling-green and some adjoining plots "buttoned down", as Dorothy Stroud puts it, "with stiff little bushes". Brown went on to draw up a plan for the full-scale remodelling of the famous Backs at Cambridge, and his drawing of 1779 for the scheme is now housed in the University Library. It is perhaps a pity that

Brown was not given the Cam to widen and the opportunity to create a smoothly unified landscape park which — and here, no doubt, was the rub — would not have stressed the boundaries of individual college grounds.

Above
In Brown's "Wilderness" at St. John's.

Below
St. John's seen from the "Wilderness".

119

CORSHAM COURT, WILTSHIRE

At Corsham Brown was employed on both house and garden, beginning in 1760. House and grounds were further altered later in the century by Repton and John Nash when they were, in effect, partners. Brown made a classical façade for the east front which looked towards his lake; this was Gothicised in 1800 by Nash. The Gothic bathhouse to the north of the house is by Brown, though Nash and Repton added the pinnacles. Dorothy Stroud quotes Brown's first estimate of December 6, 1760, which says: "To Wit the making of the great Walks and sunke Fence between the House & the Chippenham Road. The Draining the ground between the sunke Fence and the line of the garden. To making

the Water in the Parks, as also the leveling round it. The leveling round the House, as also on Front the New Building. The Sunke Fence on the Front of the Churchyard. All the Planting included Mr. Methuen to find trees and alterations which have been made in the Garden. The Above Articles comes to one Thousand and twenty Pounds."

Above
The east front of Corsham.

Below
Brown's lake at Corsham. It lies to the east of the house.

Brown's Gothic bathhouse at Corsham.

ICKWORTH, SUFFOLK

Brown worked here 1770-6 and was later consulted by the Bishop of Derry about the design of the new house begun in 1794. The Bishop's somewhat eccentric Palladian house consists of a one-hundred foot high oval rotunda from which spring two low curving wings. It was intended to hold the Bishop's splendid art collection, most of which was unfortunately lost when Napoleon occupied Rome in 1797. Capability created a serpentine road in the park at Ickworth and planted the cedars to the north of the house; and the appearance of the grounds testifies that he did much other work here.

Above left
The south side of Ickworth House. A straight gravel path, formal urns and clipped hedges.

Above right
The same path seen from the house. Beyond the steps in the middle distance can be seen the clump-planting of the eighteenth century landscape park.

Below
Clump-planting at Ickworth.

HEVENINGHAM HALL, SUFFOLK

In 1781 James Wyatt took over as architect in charge of alterations at Heveningham from Sir Robert Taylor, who had been responsible for the imposing Palladian façade of the house. In the same year Capability Brown was called in to design the park and gardens. His work here is well-preserved and, in its simplicity, Heveningham is one of his most pleasing creations. Brown set the mansion on a rising sweep of turf, masking the stables with trees, the formal gardens at the rear with their dark evergreens and geometric gravel walks and the kitchen garden, where he decided upon the crinkle-crankle wall. Brown's designs for Heveningham, still displayed in the house, show that he had more elaborate plans for the manipulation of the stream, but from springs within the grounds he finally created a most satisfying irregular, smooth-banked lake. The fine Orangery set by the cedar trees near Brown's kitchen garden is by Wyatt.

Above
Sir Robert Taylor's façade at Heveningham. Brown took the grass right up to the house.

Below
Heveningham across the lake. A fine example of Brown's manner.

Overleaf
Heveningham across the lake.

Top
James Wyatt's Orangery at Heveningham.

Above
Brown's crinkle-crankle wall in Heveningham's kitchen garden.

Opposite
Bradgate Park, the eyecatcher seen on the skyline.

BRADGATE PARK, LEICESTERSHIRE

The late eighteenth century eyecatcher, consisting of a tower and Gothic arch, is but one landscape feature at Bradgate Park in Leicestershire. The park has evolved over many centuries, never having felt the plough since the Norman conquest, and it contains a variety of landscape effects, ranging from great open sweeps with clumps of trees, reminiscent of the school of Brown, to the rougher outlines of the Picturesque.

Opposite
Bradgate, the park.

Above
Bradgate, a view of the park.

NUNEHAM COURTENAY, OXFORDSHIRE

The grounds at Nuneham are a demonstration of the variety possible in the eighteenth century landscape garden. Much had already been done when Capability Brown was consulted both as architect and gardener in 1778, and it had been eighteen years since the first Earl Harcourt moved the whole village of Nuneham away from the proximity of the house, much to Oliver Goldsmith's disgust. It was this earl who also replaced the Gothic parish church with a domed classical temple in 1764, making it one of the first churches to be created as a garden ornament. The temple served its ornamental purpose well, but apparently it was impractical in its seating arrangements for parishioners, who no longer had a church on their doorstep after 1760. The dome was unable to accommodate the old church's peal of bells, and a man ringing a handbell round the village on Sunday mornings was the unsatisfactory result of this deficiency.

The flower-garden of the poet William Mason was already seven years old when Brown came to Nuneham. Its romantic smallness and enclosure, its literary allusions, statues and bowers, and, of course, its flowers, make Mason's garden a striking contrast to Brown's open sweeps. The flower-garden once contained busts of such men as Cowley, Cato, Locke and Rousseau. The latter's romantic, sentimental feeling for the Elysian garden had its effect upon Mason's creation, as is made clear by the inscription from Rousseau on a garden seat at Nuneham: *"Si l'Auteur de la Nature est grand dans les grandes choses, il est tres grand dans les petites."* Mason's Bower, now transferred to the site of his Orangery, contains a verse from Marvell's *The Garden* which explains the emotional appeal of Mason's garden, and the inscribed urn serves the same purpose.

In 1787 William Whitehead, the Poet Laureate, published a poem entitled *The Late Improvements at Nuneham,* a dialogue between Capability Brown and the personification of Nature, in which the latter is aggrieved at Brown's success in rivalling and improving her. The poem is a tribute to Brown, to whom Whitehead gives the following words:

Who thinn'd, and who grouped, and who scattered those trees
Who bade the slopes fall with that delicate ease,
Who cast them in shade, and who placed them in light
Who bade them divide, and who bade them unite?
The ridges are melted, the boundaries are gone;
Observe all these changes, and candidly own
I have cloath'd you when naked, and when o'erdrest
I have stripped you again to your boddice and vest.

Despite the fact that the ha-ha at Nuneham has become virtually a hedge and despite the ragged appearance of the trees near the house, not to mention the distant pylons and signs of industry, the westward vista across the Thames is still recognisably and impressively Brown's. So too is the reverse view, from across the Thames to the house. The turf does not quite reach the house front now, for in the nineteenth century William Sawrey Gilpin created a rose garden and terrace adjoining this face. The serpentine Thames at Nuneham served Brown at least as well as the Cherwell had served Kent at Rousham. The plantation at the south end of the house is Brown's, and through it runs a path still known as Brown's Walk.

Above
The east front at Nuneham. Brown designed the wings, one of which is seen on the right of this picture; they are joined to the central block of the house by curving corridors.

The classical church at Nuneham. Built in 1764, it once served
as both parish church and garden ornament.

FAIR QUIET, HAVE I FOUND THEE HERE,
WITH INNOCENCE THY SISTER DEAR!
YOU SACRED PLANTS, AT LENGTH I KNOW
WILL ONLY IN RETIREMENT GROW;
SOCIETY IS ALL BUT RUDE
TO THIS DELICIOUS SOLITUDE
WHERE ALL THE FLOWERS AND TREES DO CLOSE
TO WEAVE THE GARLAND OF REPOSE.

Top
Mason's Bower at Nuneham. The classical church can be seen behind the wall.

Above
Lines from Marvell's *The Garden* inscribed on a marble tablet in Mason's Bower.

Top
Nuneham from the south-west as it was in the eighteenth century.

Above
Nuneham seen across the Thames.

HUMPHRY REPTON (1752–1818)

Humphry Repton (1752–1818) was Brown's most notable successor. He took much from the master, though he did not follow Brown in banishing terrace and parterre from the immediate proximity of the house. As a rule he preferred rustic naturalism in the small buildings that ornamented his parks and he made little use of such features as artificial ruins. For his clients, Repton would prepare books bound in red vellum outlining his projected improvements. The text would be attractively illustrated with his own water colours, and by pasting flaps over some of them Repton could show in one picture the site as it stood and, with the flap

lifted, the way he would make it look. To have had one of Repton's Red Books in one's house, even if the designs were never carried out, would certainly have been a mark of social distinction. It was pleasing to Repton that he was not just successful, but fashionable too. Confirmation of his status can be found in Jane Austen's *Mansfield Park* (1814) where Repton's name tends to occur whenever the subject of gardening is raised. For example, Mr. Rushworth exclaims in chapter six: `` 'Smith's place is the admiration of all the country; and it was a mere nothing before Repton took it in hand. I think I shall have Repton.' ''

WENTWORTH WOODHOUSE, YORKSHIRE

An example of Repton's technique of showing "before" and "after" views of the same scene. His work at Wentworth was intended to correct the "want of connexion and harmony" which he thought characterised the grounds.

135

WEST WYCOMBE, BUCKINGHAMSHIRE

When Repton came to West Wycombe the landscape park around the Palladian mansion, built mid-century for Sir Francis Dashwood, was already well formed. A nineteenth century guide-book tells us: "The gardens were ... profusely ornamented with statues, vases, temples, &c.; but most of these superfluous appendages have been removed, and the present arrangement of the pleasure grounds is by Repton." Nicholas Revett, who designed the distinctive colonnade along the south side of the house, also created the Temple of Music on the island from which Repton removed some of the trees.

Above
The east front at West Wycombe. Nicholas Revett's two storied colonnade can be seen on the south front. The parish church, topped by a large golden globe, serves as an "eyecatcher" on the richly wooded horizon.

Below
A statue of a recumbent figure overlooking the cascade which runs from the lake at West Wycombe.

Repton's suggestion for improving the landscape at West Wycombe Park, where he was employed by Sir John Dashwood in 1800.

Above
Revett's Music Temple on the island in West Wycombe's swan-shaped lake.

Opposite above
A path by the haha at West Wycombe. The haha usually disguises a boundary, but here urns draw attention to it.

Opposite below
One of the temples that remains in the once "profusely ornamented" gardens. It stands at the end of the path.

SHERINGHAM HALL, NORFOLK

Repton rightly felt that Sheringham was his masterpiece. It is difficult to imagine a more ideal English landscape setting than this where, before Repton ever touched it, Abbott Upcher had decided to make his home, anticipating "scenes of rational yet heartfelt pleasure . . . in the lovely Sheringham". The Sheringham Red Book (1812), pleasing in its stress upon the importance of not isolating the great house from the life of the village, tells that this place had "more of what my predecessor called *Capabilities*" than anywhere encountered by Repton in fifty years. His son John designed the "Grecian" house, while Repton himself commonsensically kept park and house garden separate with a modest wrought-iron fence and forbore converting cornfields into Brown-like sweeps of turf. It is possible that the temple suggested for the grounds in Repton's Red Book, never erected in the nineteenth century, may yet be built at Sheringham.

Above
Sheringham from the south-west.

Pages 142-143
The "Grecian" house at Sheringham seen from across the lake.

Top
Repton's fence dividing house garden from park at Sheringham.

Above
The park at the front of the house.

ATTINGHAM PARK, SHROPSHIRE

Repton's Red Book for Attingham, produced 1797-8, gives us an example of the way in which he would sometimes appeal to his clients' pride of ownership — rather too readily in the view of Sir Uvedale Price, who attacked the Brunonian and Reptonian landscape in his *Essay on the Picturesque* (1794). At Attingham Repton wished to build a lodge on each side of the public highway in order to suggest that the park was of greater extent than it actually was. Fourteenth in Repton's list of the causes of pleasure in landscape gardening, included in his *Enquiry* (1806), is "*Appropriation*. A word ridiculed by Mr. Price as coined by me, to describe the extent of property; yet the appearance and display of such extent is a source of pleasure not to be disregarded . . . The pleasure of appropriation is gratified in viewing a landscape which cannot be injured by the malice or bad taste of a neighbouring intruder: thus an ugly barn, a ploughed field, or any obtrusive object which disgraces the scenery of a park, looks as if it belonged to another, and therefore robs the mind of the pleasure derived from appropriation, or the unity and continuity of unmixed

property." On a small scale Repton performed an act of "appropriation" with his own cottage garden in Hare Street, Essex, where he spread his garden to include some of the public road.

The lie of the land at Attingham was not promising owing largely to its flatness, but by a judicious planting of trees and by reconstructing the flow and breadth of the river, Repton was able to create a landscape setting suitable for the mansion on which his partner Nash was employed. Repton's alteration of the river Tern meant the building of two weirs, and he succeeded in involving both the fine Tern and Atcham bridges in his landscape design — a piece of artistic "appropriation".

Above
Attingham Park. It was unpromisingly flat and barren when Repton began here.

Below
Repton did a considerable amount of planting at Attingham.